P9-EMH-931

Peck
Slither
AND Slide

SUSE MACDONALD

Gulliver Books
Harcourt Brace & Company

San Diego   New York   London

Copyright © 1997 by Suse MacDonald

Requests for permission to make copies of any part of the work
should be mailed to: Permissions Department, Harcourt Brace & Company,
6277 Sea Harbor Drive, Orlando, Florida 32887-6777.

Gulliver Books is a registered trademark of Harcourt Brace & Company.

Library of Congress Cataloging-in-Publication Data
MacDonald, Suse.
Peck, slither and slide/Suse MacDonald.
p.   cm.
"Gulliver Books."
Summary: Features animals, each matched with a verb conveying
something about the animal's behavior, accompanied by illustrations allowing
the viewer to solve the visual puzzle depicted. Includes a glossary.
ISBN 0-15-200079-8
1. Animals—Miscellanea—Juvenile literature.
[1. Animals—Miscellanea.   2. Picture puzzles.]   I. Title.
QL49.M1524   1997
591—dc20   96-18439

First edition
A C E F D B

Printed in Singapore

To Liz, my wonderful editor, who nudges me out of my comfortable corners yet honors my desire to see differently

And to Jude, who's always there when I need her

Beaver

Elephant

Flamingo

Slide

Penguin

Swing

Ape

Leopard

Slither

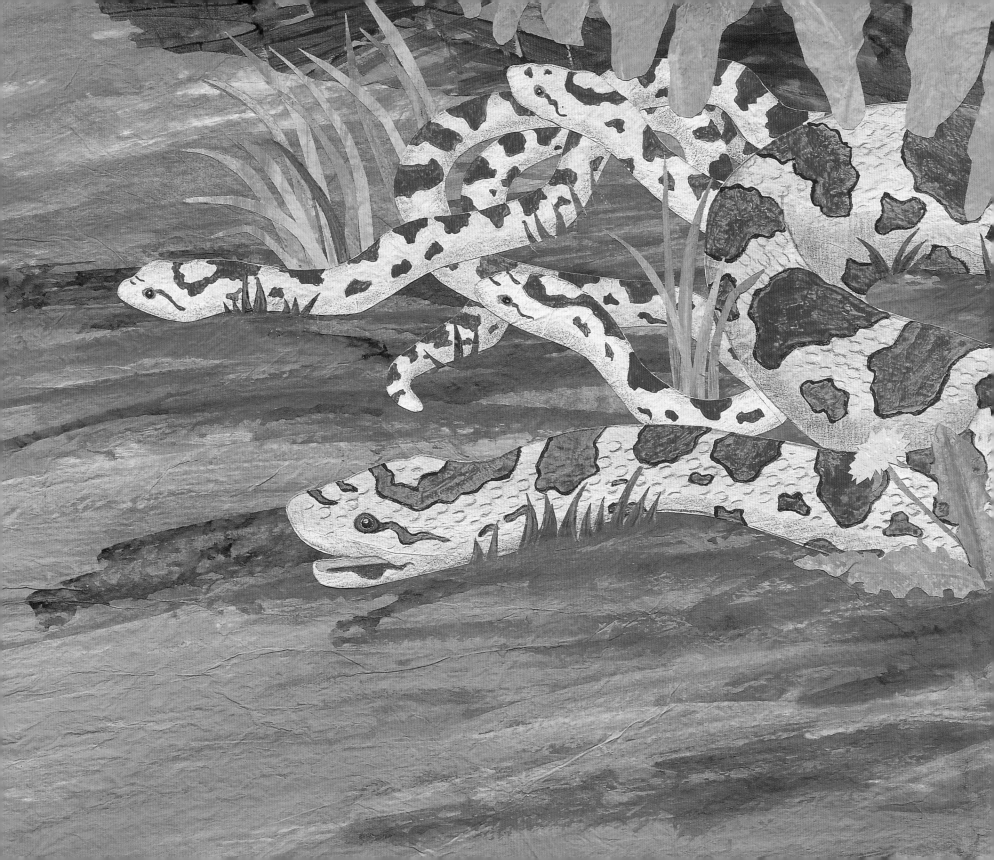

Snake

Giraffe

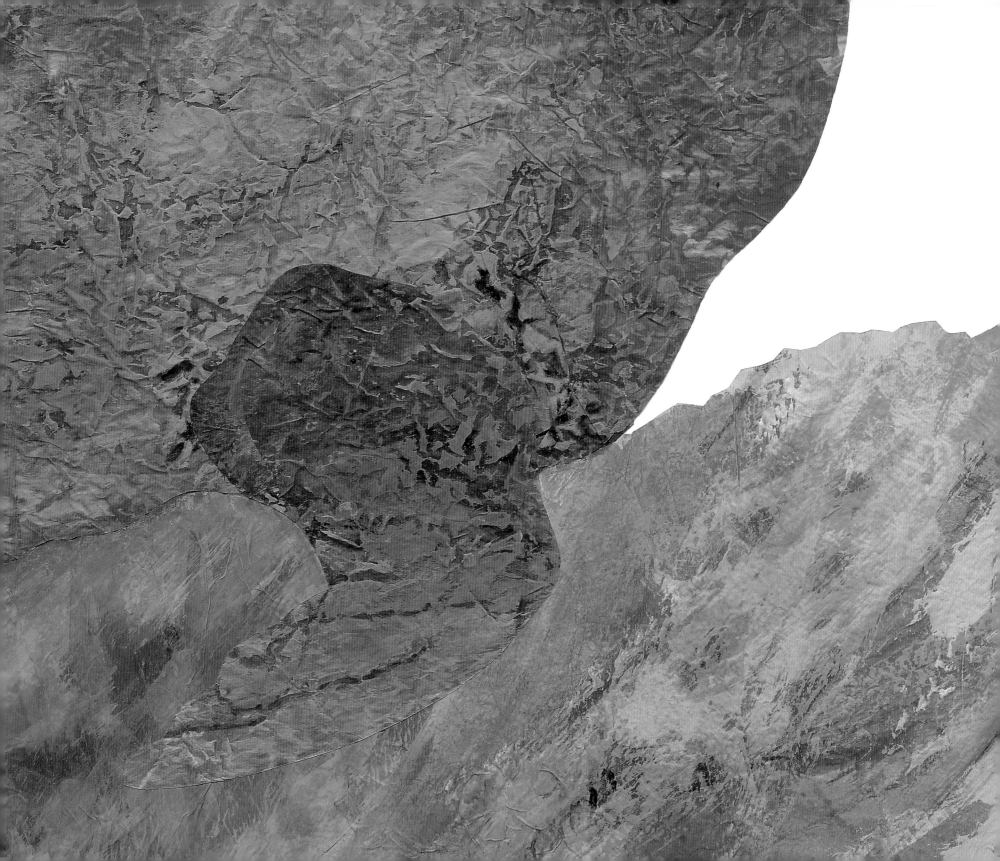

climb

Walrus

Peck

Woodpecker

Animal Facts

North American beavers can weigh up to 60 or 70 pounds and are among the largest of rodents. Beavers live near waterways surrounded by dense growths of trees. They have thick fur that provides waterproofing and insulation; forepaws that they use like hands; and large, webbed hind feet that help them swim. They can close off their ears and nostrils with special muscles when they are underwater, allowing them to stay submerged for up to fifteen minutes. Beavers gnaw through trees with their big, chisel-like front teeth to knock them down. Then they eat the bark, twigs, roots, and leaves and use the branches to build their homes. For safety, beavers commonly build their lodges on an island in the middle of a pond. If no pond exists, they create one by building a dam of mud and branches across a stream. Beaver lodges have one room above the water level, but the door is underwater to protect the beavers from predators. They also dig canals at the edges of the pond or stream, which they use to float small trees and branches to their work sites.

African elephants have larger ears and tusks than Asian elephants, and live in the forests, grasslands, and river valleys of Africa. They stand as tall as 13 feet and weigh up to 12,000 pounds. Elephants are social animals. They live in herds and use their trunks to greet, caress, and touch one another. The elephant's trunk is also its most important tool—it is used to pick up food, to detect scents, and to breathe. Elephants can fence and spar with their trunks, or warn others of danger by trumpeting through them. They eat between 500 and 1,000 pounds of vegetation a day and drink huge amounts of water by sucking it into their trunks and then squirting it into their mouths. Female elephants give birth every two to four years. Baby elephants nurse with their trunks, sucking up to $2\frac{1}{2}$ gallons of milk a day for at least two years.

Flamingos are large birds with long legs and webbed feet that are especially good for wading. They wade in shallow water, eating algae and shellfish that live in the bottom mud. When feeding, flamingos place their heads and bills upside down below the surface of the water. Using their tongues, they suck in water and mud and then push it out again past the notched edges of their bills. When the water and mud flow out, the algae and shellfish get trapped inside the birds' mouths. It is because these food sources vary that flamingos range in color from pale pink to bright red. Pigments in the food pass into their bodies and through to their feathers, affecting their color. Flamingos live in large colonies throughout the Caribbean, Africa, Southern Asia, Europe, and South America. They build round nests made of mud and lay their eggs in a shallow depression at the top of the nest. Males and females take turns sitting on the eggs, and the young hatch in about a month.

Emperor penguins live in the coldest part of the southern hemisphere, the Antarctic Ocean. They are the largest of the eighteen species of penguins and live in huge colonies that may have as many as several million birds. Penguins cannot fly. Instead, they swim, using their wings as flippers in the water. On snow and ice, they either walk upright on their feet or, using their flippers to push off, slide on their bellies. Penguins' bodies are covered with tiny, waterproof feathers that keep them warm and dry. They spend most of their time in the water, hunting for fish and squid to eat. The female penguin lays one egg on the ice and then immediately returns to the sea. The male penguin keeps the egg warm for two months by balancing it on his feet and covering it with a flap of feathered skin. Once the chick has hatched, the mother comes back to care for it and the father dives into the sea to feed. When he returns, the parents care for their chick together.

Apes and monkeys are both primates, but apes are larger than monkeys and have no tails. The ape family includes gorillas, chimpanzees, orangutans, and gibbons (pictured here), which are the smallest members. Gibbons stand up to 3 feet tall, weigh as much as 28 pounds, and have long arms and legs. They live in the tops of trees in the forests of Southeast Asia and rarely come down to the ground. They use their long arms to swing from branch to branch in search of a meal. When they find their favorite foods they hang from the branches to eat. They mostly feed on figs, mangos, grapes, plums, and other fruit, but they also like leaves, insects, and occasionally birds and birds' eggs. Gibbons sleep in trees, curling up on the limbs. A mother gives birth every two to three years. Each baby is raised by its mother until it is one or sometimes two years old. Then the father takes over and teaches his youngster how to swing through the trees.

Leopards are large cats that live in the forests, grasslands, and swamps of Africa, Asia, and the Middle East. They grow to be as big as 6½ feet in length. Their fur is usually a brownish-yellow color with dark brown or black spots. This coloring makes them hard to see in long grass and trees and helps them to hide while eating or sleeping. Leopards are good swimmers and climbers and spend a lot of time in trees. They sleep on the limbs and often eat there as well. A leopard may drag its kill into a tree by picking up the animal in its strong jaws. This keeps the cat's dinner protected from other animals that might try to steal it. Leopards usually hunt alone, both during the day and at night. They eat waterbuck, antelopes, birds, snakes, baboons, sheep, and sometimes animals that have been killed by other predators.

Eastern milk snakes are grayish tan with dark reddish-brown blotches on their backs and sides. They can be found in the northeastern United States and lower Canada. During the cold winters, they hibernate deep in caves or burrows, where the temperature stays above freezing. In the warm weather, they live in woods, meadows, and flower beds. Milk snakes hunt at night and sleep during the day. They eat frogs, fish, earthworms, slugs, lizards, rodents, and nesting birds and their eggs, but they are not dangerous to people. The snake seizes its victim around the back of the neck, behind its head, and surrounds it with several coils, squeezing it until it suffocates. The food is then consumed headfirst. Milk snakes grow to be up to 4 feet long. They slither along the ground by moving their long, slender bodies in loops from side to side. By pushing against the ground with the loops of their bodies, they propel themselves forward.

Giraffes live in the semi-arid plains of Africa, south of the Sahara. They are the tallest animals in the world, reaching almost 20 feet in height and weighing up to 2,000 pounds. Giraffes feed on the leaves, buds, and fruits of acacia and thorn trees. Their long necks enable them to reach the leaves at the tops of trees, leaving those at the bottom for smaller animals. Giraffes' height also enables them to spot predators at a great distance, and with their long legs they can run at speeds of up to 30 miles an hour. One baby giraffe, called a calf, is born to a mother every two years or so. It is born while the mother is standing, and it drops to the ground unhurt. The calves weigh 100 to 250 pounds and stand about 6 feet tall at birth. A calf nurses for around six months and continues to grow for about ten years.

Walruses live in the cold regions of the Arctic Ocean, swimming in the water and resting on rocky islands or on the ice floating above shellfish beds. Walruses can grow close to 12 feet long and weigh nearly 3,000 pounds. They have heavy tusks and four flippers. Both the flippers and the tusks help them climb onto the ice and rocks where they rest. They are very clumsy on land and move slowly, sometimes just dragging themselves along with their strong front flippers. Walruses are more graceful in the water, where they use their flippers for swimming and diving. They dive down to the shellfish beds to feed on clams and other creatures that live there. They also feed on fish, starfish, and sometimes even mammals. Walrus females give birth to one baby every two years or so. The babies weigh about 130 pounds at birth and stay with their mothers for up to two years.

Pileated woodpeckers are found in heavily wooded areas all over North America. One of the larger types of woodpeckers, they grow to be about the size of a crow, 14 to 18½ inches tall. They have black feathers, with white stripes along the sides of the head and neck and under the wings, and a red crest on top of the head. Woodpeckers use their strong beaks to drill holes in trees in search of insects, like carpenter ants, that live inside the wood. Once they have made a hole, they use their long, sticky tongues to collect the insects and draw them into their mouths. They cling to the bark of the tree with their clawed feet, which have two toes facing forward and two facing backward. Their stiff tail feathers help brace them against the tree. Woodpeckers also build their nests in tree holes; first they peck to enlarge the hole and then they line it with wood chips.

The illustrations in this book are tissue paper colored
with acrylic paint and mounted on 100% rag illustration board.
The title type was set in Esprit Medium and the text type was set in
Avant Garde, Franklin Gothic Heavy, Belshaw, Caxton Book Italic,
Limehouse Script, Blackfriar, Neue Neuland Light, Carpenter, Willow, Birch,
and Gill Sans Bold Condensed by the Photocomposition Center,
Harcourt Brace & Company, San Diego, California.
Color separations by Bright Arts, Ltd., Singapore
Printed and bound by Tien Wah Press, Singapore
This book was printed on totally chlorine-free Nymolla Matte Art paper.
Production supervision by Stanley Redfern
Designed by Lori McThomas Buley and Suse MacDonald